SHATTERED GLASS

Starting Over And Trusting God To Put You Back Together Again

Kristal Clark

SHATTERED GLASS: Starting Over And Trusting God To Put You Back Together Again

Copyright @ 2019 by Kristal Clark
ISBN: 978-1-7326880-8-7

Printed in USA

Sparkle Publishing Company
www.sparklepublishing.net
Editors: DeVon Mays and Paula McFadden Norris
Cover Design: Annie Marek-Barta

Creative Content Editor:
Sharenda Williams, VIA Consulting
www.viaconsulting.live

Unless otherwise note, all biblical references used are from the New Living Translation (NLT) ©

Kristal has completely opened herself up to share her struggles and deepest secrets. She is refreshingly honest and relatable, and make you feel as though you're reading the book of a close friend. She will challenge you to assess your life while lovingly empowering you to deal with those dark areas that no one knows about. Truly, a necessary read for anyone who wants to be exactly who God called them to be.

-Pastor Brelyn Bowman

I have known Kristal Clark for a couple of years now, and in that small time she has not only given me the honor of mentoring her she has inspired my life also. She doesn't just speak about helping people, but she puts it in action. Her life has been lived and continues to bring joy to each person she touches. She has gone through fire, and lives to bring awareness to us all on all things abuse and human trafficking. I know her book is going to change your life because her life has changed mine.

-Pastor Cora Jakes Coleman

Kristal is a beautiful, descriptive writer who knows how to capture your heart and spirit with both truth and transparency. She eliminates the fluff by getting to the root of fragmentation. Her story is not only compelling, but it is inspirationally charged with action. She doesn't want you to merely read her story, but her approach is getting you to discover freedom in God's word. Her story will cause you to look introspectively that will nudge you towards real change. Her experiences with shattered moments will allow you to clearly see through the glass of God's grace, redemption, and love. This is a must read! Read and see for yourself!

- Dr. Estrelita Bruce,
Christian Counselor & Founder of A NEW ME:
Transparently, Abundantly, LLC

When it comes to injustice, specifically related to abuse, surely there needs to be a great sounding of the alarm. Even greater than it is happening now. Kristal Clark is just the amplification needed in this hour. In her book, Shattered Glass, she releases a refreshing measure of hope through her transparency. In reading her words, one comes to know that he or she is an overcomer as well. All are affected by abuse in some way, whether directly are indirectly. As such, I recommend this book not just for you, but also for those you know are in need of this timely tool as well.

-Yolanda Chevette Perry, Author/Speaker

Kristal Clark's transparency, authenticity, and realness in this book will bring hope and healing to people that need it most. I'm confident this book will change the way people see brokenness and respond to hurt. As a new father to a baby girl, I am especially excited to know there is a book that empowers all people, especially women to live unashamed, whole and powered by the grace of God. I am inspired!

-Dr. John Gaines

Table of Contents

Acknowledgements

To my beautiful daughter Kenadi, the sky is the limit for you baby girl.

Kacia and Kiara, you fill me with so much joy, hope, and unconditional love. My life would not be the same without you girls.

Vernon Brazzle, my father, you have set the standard high in my life, and I will never forget your fatherly love.

Annie Brazzle, my mother, you made sure that I did not go without one thing. For that, I am truly grateful.

My amazingly talented little sister, April Allen; you make me so proud. You are a powerhouse of talent.

Carla Yarborough, thank you for being a true sister to me. I love you for life!

To my RPS sisters, I love each of you dearly!

Sharenda Williams, thank you for your editorial creativity and commitment to the journey.

To my spiritual mother, Kimberly Jones-Pothier, thank you for loving me through every season of my journey. I love you BIG! You are an answer to my prayers.

Foreword

Beautifully Broken is where God does His best work. Life has taught me two things; bad things happen to good people and bad things happen to bad people. These adverse conditions can either cause you to get bitter or you can get better.

The enemy will attempt to pollute our thoughts and keep us prisoner to the shame of our secrets. He wants you to believe that you deserved everything that has happened to you. We even protect those who never protected us because of the guilt and shame of what was done to us.

Instead of dealing with our truth and getting healed for real, we place a band aid on a wound that actually required stitches. It is time for you to believe that you are WORTH being healed.

When we are not in tune with the voice of God, it becomes easy to believe the lies of the enemy. You are unwanted. There is no one fighting for you. You are not pretty, special or smart enough for anyone to ever love you as you are. These are all lies created to keep you stuck in a season for an entire lifetime. Satan does not want you or me to ever wake up to the truth that WE DIDN'T deserve what happened to us and we are enough.

If you were to ever grab hold of the real TRUTH, "hurt people hurt people but healed people heal people", it would shift the trajectory of your life. When we finally begin to release forgiveness, we gain real FREEDOM.

The worldview perspective of forgiveness feels like a pardon. If I forgive you then, you got away with what you did to me. That is so NOT TRUE!

Forgiveness is not absolution for the offender, but a gift for the victim.

Shift your perspective and think like a child of the KING. Do not get stuck, FORGIVE them so that you can MOVE FORWARD in your destiny. God has great plans for your life according to Jeremiah 29:11. But do not let one season of your life define your entire lifetime. Listen, God is a HEALER! You make the choice, to allow God the opportunity to heal you, for real.

Shift your focus from what HAPPENED to what is HAPPENING. You survived, you made it and you have the scars to prove it. I always say, "Your scars are the tattoos that show YOU MADE IT."

IIe didn't let the abuse and heartbreak happen to you, but He sure will use it and you to lead millions directly to Him. God is wanting to use every piece of your life, even the broken pieces. "All things are working together for your good," Romans 8:28.

When you become intentional about your healing and moving forward in your new future, you will not allow anyone, or anything to keep you from being healed.

I believe after reading this book, you too will experience a freedom from the pain of your past. No longer will you be moving forward looking through the rearview mirror.

The enemy has kept you bound by the shame and distraction of your past for the final day. As of today, the enemy has lost the war that he waged against your mind. This day has been a long time coming, but it is finally here. Just know this my friend, he was not fighting you because you are weak. Oh no, he was after you because you are STRONG.

Cheers to you for having the courage to begin this journey towards your own personal healing. You are not just reading another book, but you are about to find your exit strategy.

I have a front row seat to the transformation that is happening in Kristal's life. In this book, she will share her heart and healing with you. Everything you are about to read is a testament of God's amazing healing power when you give Him permission to heal you.

She did not allow her circumstances to dictate her future. Instead, she allowed God to turn her pain into purpose, her scars into stars and her mess into a message.

God is a chain breaker and you, you my friend are a game changer. The world is in need of survivors just like you. You have faced every trial with grace and humility. I am so proud of your success and most importantly, God is proud of you. Everyone has a story, but yours my daughter will be a BESTSELLER.

Kimberly "Real Talk Kim" Pothier

Pastor, Mentor, Spiritual Mom

He Heals the wounds of every shattered heart.

- Psalm 147:3

"

Shatter the glass

of any negative in your past,
remove the burden carried upon
your back, and cut the rope
from around your neck that's
attempting to choke your reality.
Stand with hope and truth to
face all trials with dignity,
breathe deep the sweet
fragrance of victory, for your
freedom is emerging from within.

Denise Marie

Introduction

Pieces, the remains of that which has been broken. Pain will break you and leave you shattered. Much like what happens when glass meets excessive force and pressure, I too have been broken. Although I have experienced several tragedies that left me in pieces, God has given me a peace that goes beyond or exceeds anything I could ever understand (Philippians 4:7, NLT). That peace has also given me the grace to be transparent and share my story of healing with every one of you reading this book.

My purpose has pain. I elected to not get bitter, but instead to get better. As you will read, the pages of my journey have been smothered with abandonment, rejection and all manners of abuse. Nonetheless, I have made the decision and given God permission to use every ounce of my suffering to win men and women to the kingdom of God. My past is not pretty, but the mess of my life is becoming the message that will release freedom to millions.

God has exchanged my pieces for His peace. The loss was significant, but His grace was and is sufficient. Guess what, pain is painful, and it will distort your view. Just like Jesus, our greatest example, while He was in pain was used to heal.

In Philippians 4:9 (NLT), the writer encourages us to, "Fix your thoughts on what is true, and honorable, and right, and pure, and lovely and admirable. Think about things that are excellent and worthy of praise." It would be easy for me to remain in pieces, but God has called us out of the broken places in our lives. He has found value in our brokenness, but we have to think like He does.

It has taken a lot of heart work to be where I am in my journey. Some days are better than others, but I am determined to defeat the enemy and live a life that is victorious and pleasing to God. The decision to write this book has forced me into a vulnerable and transparent place. As I am writing this book, my marriage of almost seventeen years has ended. Now, I have survived molestation, rape, abandonment, rejection, and most recently divorce. In the midst of all the ugliness, I choose to find the beauty.

As you are reading some of the most difficult parts of my past, my hope is for you to find the strength and the courage to endure whatever you might be facing right now. The vision for this book was to show you what God can do if you allow Him. My friend, I am a living miracle.

You might be asking, Kristal how did you overcome? Let me encourage you. The you who is walking around in guilt, shame and fear. You are not what happened to you. Keep reading. I am going to share with you the keys for unlocking healing and the next level. I encourage you to pause for the journaling segment in this book. These were intentionally included to prompt you to dig deep and seek Jesus for your healing. We got this so let's do this together.

"

She was unstoppable
not because she did not have
failures or doubts but because
she continued on despite them.

Beau Taplin

Chapter 1

Broken Pieces

Once broken always broken is a misconception and the greatest form of deception that the enemy will try and use against you. Trust me, I was once broken and shattered into many pieces. Some of those pieces were bigger than others, but God still looked at me and saw the most wonderful masterpiece. With skillful intention, he has put me back together again and again.

Let's just be honest, no one wants to walk through the pain of being in pieces. My truth is one of extreme emotional, physical and mental anguish. For the sake of my family, many of the details will be excluded.

My prayer is before you read the final word in this book, that you will have a greater understanding of my healing not my hurting. My goal is to point every reader to Jesus Christ and not have the focus be on the shattered seemingly beyond repair pieces of my life.

Both my mom and dad were pastors, so I was born into a God- loving family. While my dad provided for the family, mom took great pride and joy in raising my baby sister and me. Just like every family, we had our difficult seasons and personal struggles.

Perfection was the key to success in my home and family. Things needed to be a certain way to be right. Our outer appearance was a piece of that perfection. My sister and I often wore pretty fluffy dresses and matching sandals.

For me, this would become the beginning of my journey of abandonment and rejection.

Perfection was all about our presentation not only to God but to people. Our over exaggerated outfits were like masks worn to hide or veil the truth. It is not only hidden from others, but it is also hidden from you. As long as I do not see, I will not have to deal with it. That is an immature way of thinking.

That seed will take root and grow on the inside of you. For every seed planted, docs not matter the quality of the seed, there will be a harvest. Now you are an adult living with the harvest of a seed planted when you were just a child.

The need to be perfect became a desire to remain perfect and quickly affected all of my relationships. Perfection became about performance. Even with my parents, I did not know how to accept love from them without performing for it. Everything I did was about winning and maintaining their approval.

This excessive need for approval made me feel like an orphan. Yes, I lived in a two-parent family, but I always felt strange as a child. It was like I did not fit because I would never measure up to the standards of perfection.

So many of you reading this book probably grew up in a home very similar to mine. The constant fear of imperfection paralyzed me and my relationship with Jesus was hindered. Although grateful for an early introduction to God, my relationship with Him was birth out of some very traumatic incidents that started in my childhood.

I know I am not the only one to have this skewed version of Christianity. Tormented by my guilt of not being able to do everything the right way every time. The enemy had me right where he wanted me, engulfed in shame and disgust. For many years, I carried the burden of the molestation, multiple rapes and even my divorce.

My response to it all was a numbness that infused my body. I felt nothing and there was no apparent hope of joy. Mom taught my sister and me that everything God created was beautiful. What she failed to teach us was that beautiful things can be broken. However, it does not erase the beauty of what He created. In fact, Beautifully Broken is where God does His best work. This is when you allow God into your broken places to start the healing process.

The testimony of my journey is painful, but it was all about the process and getting to this very moment of healing so that I can share my struggles and successes with you all. You my friend have two choices. You can remain a broken mess or you can choose to give God permission to restore the broken pieces of your life. He can and will use your mess as a message turning your scars into stars.

Use your pain as promotion not as an excuse to remain in a season of your life. That is all this is, a season not a sentence. My spiritual mother always says, "Kristal, if you have a pulse God has a plan." Although death was an option, I choose every single day to live. There have been days that life has knocked me flat on my back, but I do not stay there, I roll over and become face down crying out to the God of my salvation.

The enemy will give you a false sense of security in this norm. I am a visual being so allow me to explain how I see the tactics of the enemy. Your brokenness is like a room that has been properly adorned and furnished to keep you there. Have you ever been on a vacation, entered your hotel room and said these words, "I will not have to leave for anything"?

The property manager has gone above and beyond to meet the expectations of the guests. In this example, the enemy is the property manager of your broken pieces. He has painted the walls with temporary JOY. It is furnished with plots and plans to keep you distracted and stuck in a place that was designed to be transient. While you are in this well-furnished and decorated room, SHAME is stealing your focus and keeping you silent, unable to SPEAK life into your brokenness. The amenities in this room were designed specifically with the expectations that the truth of your pain will cause you to remain hidden.

As of today, you are under new management. Your healing is just on the other side of your revealing. The mask of perfection can keep you hidden from your destiny. Presenting your broken pieces to God will open doors providing a way of escape from what the enemy wants to create as your norm. This norm was designed to keep you handcuffed and chained to your past and to delay you from this truth, **"If the Son therefore shall make you free, ye shall be free indeed" (John 8:36, KJV).**

Bad things happen to us, while God uses them for good and allows them to happen for us. This revelation has changed my life forever.

I am not what happened to me. Those are labels I was not designed to wear. My view of who God really is has been changed. His love for me goes beyond my wildest dreams and my hope is renewed.

Brokenness does not discriminate against its victim. Pray that God will reveal the broken pieces in your life. Recall those broken pieces in your life and write them here. Trust that God is healing you in the revealing.

"If the Son therefore shall make you free, ye shall be free indeed" (John 8:36, KJV).

As you pray, begin to write what God speaks to you about your freedom.

_____

_____

_____

_____

_____

_____

_____

_____

_____

_____

_____

_____

_____

"

You can't go back and change
the beginning but you can
start where you are and

change the ending.

C.S. Lewis

Chapter 2
Fragments of A Shattered Voice

Fragment-an odd piece, bit, or scrap

God wants us to be whole, nothing missing, and nothing broken. However, life has a way of breaking us. We go through problems and experience pains that will shake us to our very core. Yet God is standing with His arms opened wide, welcoming us with our broken pieces in tow, fragments of what is our lives.

Molestation, rape, emotional abuse and divorce are the fragments that I present to Him daily. These things came to shatter my voice and to silence the purpose of God.

When something is broken, its value is often lost. But God will take the fragments of our lives and restore value. "All things are working together for my good." That includes the sexual assaults and the divorce. Absolutely everything that I have endured and will encounter.

The objective of the enemy is to silence the victim. At the age of four, I was molested by my god sister. Smiling at me the entire time, she told me not to tell anyone. There were no threats, just a request to be silent.

This one experience changed my life forever. It seemed as though it placed a mark on me that told abusers that I was the perfect victim. My silence was an all access pass for bad things to happen to me.

What she had done to me was despicable and indescribable. I became physically ill, but yet I refused to break the silence. My offender was seemingly winning, and I was apparently losing. The lenses by which I viewed the world were now fogged and my vision was blurry. My silence kept me vulnerable to the abuse and the abuser. After all, my mom trusted her mother completely. My silence protected everyone except for me.

I would often wonder if there were something internally wrong with me that attracted terrible people. Oh how I wish I could say there was only one count of sexual abuse, but there were more. When I was eleven years old, my teacher molested me. It was after this brutal violation that I decided to break the silence. Finally, I was done with being mute.

Finding the courage to stand up and speak out was not easy. Although painful, the silence was comfortable. It gave me a place to hide from the ugly truth of what had happened to me and what was currently happening.

Allow me to encourage you, give your voice some volume. You do not have to remain silent when you are being abused and violated. It does not matter if it had the hands of a stranger or someone you know and love. Silence will strip you of your power, but when you open your mouth that power is restored.

My decision to speak up, quite possibly saved the life of another young girl. Even today, God has given me a voice for the broken. My organization, Rock Paper Scissors (RPS), was founded as a result of the pain I suffered to help others who are suffering. The devil knows we have a great future and he will do all that he can to keep us silent.

God is a healer. Not only does He want to heal you, but He wants to make you whole again. That can only happen if you place the fragments of your life in His hands. Most of the time we want to hold onto the other parts and present to Him what is becoming or beautiful. Truthfully, all that we are without Him is nothing at all. Apart from Him, we have no value to boast about.

Those fragments that you present to Him will be refurbished and their value restored. Sometimes we want another person to help us put our life back together and we cut them. Only God can pick up the shattered glass and not get cut. When He puts His hands on our shattered pieces, they instantly become whole.

You are worthy of His restoration and being loved. Whatever has happened to you was not your fault. As scary as it was to confess the abuse, my voice started to give my eyes sight. For the first time in a long time, I felt the power of God. Being raised in a preacher's home, I understood the presence of God and how important it was in our lives even at the age of eleven.

The bad things, however, did not stop. For a while though, I was on track to a normal life. I had friends and was even dating. High school alone is a challenge for someone like me. Then it happened again, the guy I was dating raped me. Suddenly my normal became a hellish nightmare and I became like a hamster on a wheel. It was like his violation restarted a cycle of abuse that I could not escape. The best way to define my life was insanity.

Here I am again. Do I speak up or remain silent? It seemed as if neither had worked out for me in the past. I stayed silent and it happened, I spoke up and it happened.

Fast forward many years and I am now a wife, mother and mentor to women all over the United States. Although I am giving a voice to the silent, my silence has returned.

My marriage was broken and there was no restoration in site. Instead of admitting that we were at the brink of no return, we continued living our lives jointly separate. I was clinging with all my might to the hope that things would get better, or that things would just click again.

Daily I prayed for a miracle to happen in my marriage. The last thing I wanted was to subject my daughter to our broken mess. Yet here we were buried deep in the fragments of a dysfunctional relationship.

Divorce is not what I wanted but being stuck in something that was not real was not fair to our daughter either. From the moment God blessed us with her, all I wanted was to be able to give my daughter a whole family, something I felt I lacked. Although my parents never separated or divorced, they were split by their hearts.

We too were living in the same cycle of dysfunction. Our marriage had no true foundation and we were together for appearances only. After sixteen and a half years of marriage I had to accept our truth, we were getting divorced.

The reality of it all created emotions that hit me like an avalanche. Everyone would know that I was facing a devastating tragedy. My actions at attempting to save my marriage were unhealthy and in turn caused me more pain.

The desperation to maintain this marriage had consumed me and to finally have to release it was like losing a piece of my identity. Here was yet another fragment that I was presenting to God. The mask I had worn for so many years was coming off.

It felt like I had failed my daughter, myself and most important God. The feelings of hopelessness coupled with shame and abandonment literally brought me to my knees in total surrender. While on my knees God spoke to my broken heart, "What happens when the ring comes off? That is not your identity. Your identity is found in me."

"I hear you Lord but help me to live out those words."

Understand that my entire life was about presenting a perfect version of me to a God who knows we are not perfect. God's plans for us is perfect even when we are not. His love for us comes with no strings attached.

As difficult as it was to accept my new reality, I realized that God was calling me out of a toxic relationship and environment. When something is toxic it is poisonous and can be lethal. The enemy tried to use this situation to kill me physically, emotionally and financially. Guess who is getting the last laugh? Me.e.

What the enemy meant for evil God has turned it around for my good. No weapon formed against me shall prosper and I am more than a conqueror through Christ Jesus.

God reminded me of my true identity. It is not rooted in a ring, marital status or even another human being. I have walked through some difficult seasons, but I am still standing firmly on the word of God. What the enemy contrived to kill, steal and destroy did not work.

Ask yourselves, "what happens when the ring comes off?" I can tell you from personal experience that God has a plan for your life. Learn to trust Him and seek Him even in your brokenness. You are never too broken to cry out to the savior. He died to hear this very prayer.

"The well does not need a physician." God has come for the sick and diseased. It is by His stripes that we are healed. The healing is not just for physical ailments but emotional sickness.

God is concerned about everything that concerns you. **"Casting all your care upon Him, because He cares for you," (I Peter 5:7, KJV, emphasis added).** There is nothing to insignificant to take to the throne of grace. He desires that we become exclusively dependent upon Him.

Metaphorically, "What happens when the ring comes off?" What will happen when you have to reveal your broken fragments to your friends, family and church members?

_____

_____

_____

_____

_____

_____

_____

_____

_____

_____

_____

_____

_____

_____

_____

You might not be ready or able to confront the person(s) but take the time right now and get real with yourself. What areas in your life have you remained silent or do you continue to remain silent?

_____

_____

_____

_____

_____

_____

_____

_____

_____

_____

_____

_____

_____

_____

For I know the plans I have for you declares the Lord, plans to prosper you and not to harm you. Plans to give you hope and a future. -Jeremiah 29:11

"

There will be periods of bliss
and there will be periods of
excruciatingly uncomfortable
growth. The goals isn't to control
the process and avoid the
discomfort. The goal is to
surrender to the growth and
appreciate the bliss within the
discomfort.

Trust the process.

Kathrin Zenkina

Chapter 3
Shards of Shame & Denial

This is probably going to be the hardest chapter that I share with you all. Denial, it is not a great place to dwell, be a tourist or even have a layover. Until about three years ago, I was living as a full-time resident. I honestly thought that we or I could remain in a marriage that was repeating a cycle in my life. Although in my heart I knew the truth, but my actions refused to admit the truth of my heart. I prayed daily for the Lord to restore my marriage. Every time I thought we were on the path of healing, there was another shard of brokenness unveiled.

One day I realized, I was not leaving because I wanted this marriage to work, I was staying because my pride had been bruised. It was easier for my appearance to remain in a faux marriage. In my mind, the platform required that I privately endure the pain and the reality of my crumbling life.

Suddenly a shift happened in my mind. The blinders came off and I started to see what was real. I was no longer in denial about my marriage but now I was in denial about dealing with the fall out of my failed marriage.

For so long the enemy had tormented me and made me feel like a complete failure. He constantly reminded me of all the things I had done wrong. He also made me feel guilty for the things that had happened to me that were completely out of my control.

Shame and denial are partners in keeping you stuck. These are the tactics and strategies that the enemy will use trying to make sure that you do not experience freedom.

Have you ever looked up the definition of denial in the dictionary? Webster describes it like this, "the action of declaring something untrue." Denial is a physical action, and you make the choice to tell yourself or others that something is not true. Isn't it wild to think that it takes more effort to even just believe a lie than speak the truth?

If you also look up the definition of truth, it reads, "the quality or state of being true." So, when you stay in denial, there is actual work to just stay there, to stop yourself from moving forward and believing that this isn't all there is. It says so in the actual definition of denial: "action" but with truth, it's a "quality or state of being." So, we are exerting more precious energy in keeping ourselves in denial, because we must take action in declaring something is untrue. Whereas truth is a state of being, there's no work. Okay, Webster's dictionary, I see you.

There is freedom in the truth. It explains the struggle I had been in when I came to the realization that many times in my life, I was in denial and not moving forward. Abuse can do that to you, but also a lack of intentionality can do that to you. The Bible has a very specific story on what happens when you are in denial, and you allow denial to grow. The Israelites were stuck in the wilderness for 40 years. What was meant to be a stop along the way became their destination by their choices. Have you ever wanted something so badly that you put "blinders" on and chose to only see what you wanted to? That is a form of being in denial–choosing not to focus on the entirety of your situation.

The Israelites were scared to migrate into the Promised Land because they feared the unknown and doubted God's plan. I kept fighting for a union that wasn't blessed by God in the beginning. I diluted my faith and I acted as if I didn't see or feel certain things in my relationship. Instead of having the hard conversations and stopping myself to do an inventory of how things really were going because I didn't want the pain, I found myself walking around the situation instead of walking through it and really arriving at the truth.

I remember thinking, "God, you can touch this part of my life over here but not my relationship because it's going to sting too badly if I don't get the reaction that I need." So, I put blinders on to see only what I wanted to see. And in my organization, I've always had passion for the work God has given me, always.

I came to realize how much denial I was in and how denial created an avalanche in my life. After having this realization because of my marriage ending, I just became so exasperated with myself. And that is how breakthrough is born. God takes your feelings of exhaustion from fighting, and the minute you surrender, He's able to come in and do His good work.

I had to start shifting my thoughts to focusing on how this will be new—and how after death, there is always life. A life with Jesus Christ is the promise of this. I realized that I had to become so exhausted and out of options so that God could reveal to me that it was my decision to stay in denial, that I was keeping myself from seeing what He has for me. I had to face it. I had to call it out, to recognize what it was in order for me to deal with it and really focus on what I should be focusing on that is the truth.

Recognizing denial is crucial because it will break you free from negative and crippling thoughts. Living in truth leads to deeper healing and allows you to be intentional in an area that has been neglected or overlooked. And what happens after is a shift in perspective, a growth in your own personal awareness and glimpses of God's will for your life.

It is the bigger picture and this big picture will look different for everyone. For me, it was letting go of denial and really embracing the new journey ahead of me, focusing on my healing. Remembering that with death and the end of something, Jesus brings life and wholeness and healing because His word says that He works ALL things out for our good: not some, not a little, but ALL.

"And I know that nothing good lives in me, that is, in my sinful nature. I want to do what is right, but I can't." (Romans 7:18) How does this verse encourage you to be willing to forgive yourself and others?

What areas in your life are you feeling stuck in denial? Write as many that comes to your mind. What are the reasons that you remain in denial?

_____

_____

_____

_____

_____

_____

_____

_____

_____

_____

_____

_____

_____

_____

_____

_____

"

**Denial is the worst kind of lie
because it is the lie you**
tell yourself.

Michelle A. Homme

Chapter 4

Fragments of Forgiveness

What is forgiveness? Let me first tell you what it is not. Forgiveness is not developing amnesia and living like what happened to you was not real. Let's just be honest sis, you were wounded, but you do not have to remain that way. Forgiveness does not recuse the offender from their responsibility; however, it will free you from the bondage of being controlled by the offense.

Forgiveness is a choice that only you can make. Your future is predicated on your decision to let go of feelings of bitterness, anger and the need for revenge. The unwillingness to forgive can prove detrimental to your spirit life as well as your emotional wellbeing. You think you are hurting them when in truth you are hurting yourself and limiting the favor of God in your own life.

There is a quote by the late Dr. Martin Luther King Jr. that made a lasting impression on my heart. "Forgiveness is not an occasional act, it is a constant attitude."

Those words blew me away when I first read them. We limit forgiveness to an act when it is actually an attitude. The struggle to forgive could be related to this very quote. We are trying to only forgive when it is easy or expected. There will be days and times when forgiveness will be difficult, seemingly undeserved and very much unexpected.

Peter inquires of Jesus, "how often should I forgive my neighbor, seven times a day? Jesus replied, seventy times seven a day." This scripture seals the end of Dr. King's quote. Forgiveness is a *constant* attitude.

As I am writing this book, I am surviving divorce and walking in true forgiveness. First, I had to make the choice to forgive myself and then forgive those who had harmed me both intentionally and unintentionally. Everyone will not be able to walk that path so quickly. It is not because I am or want to be better and more spiritual than anyone else.

My goal every day is to be a better me than I was on yesterday. In my own nature, I would not have been able to walk in this type of holistic forgiveness. **"And I know that nothing**

good lives in me, that is, in my sinful nature. I want to do what is right, but I can't" **(Romans 7:18, NLT).** There is nothing good inside of me that is of myself. All the good in me is from God.

To be completely honest, I did not think I could or would. When the injury first takes place, all you can think about is revenge. How can I get them back for what they have done to me? You are only wanting that person to hurt as much as you do at that very moment. Forgiveness, seemingly, would release them of any guilt, shame, or pain.

There are so many advantages to being willing to forgive. I will share briefly with you three that have been most relatable to me in my life. Healthier relationships, mental health and physical health were benefits of my decision to walk the path of forgiveness. This was not just for my ex-spouse, but my parents, the boyfriends, and my God sister. Let's jump right in and learn why forgiveness was the best choice for me.

Forgiveness promotes healthier relationships. My marriage produced my beautiful daughter. She is the love of my life and I would lose mine if it meant she could have her life for a second longer. God allowed me to understand that my forgiveness was for me primarily but also for her. She and I share a resemblance, but she also has many traits like her father. Hating him is like hating her. I never, ever want to hate any part of my daughter.

Many of you may be familiar with my non-profit organization, Rock Paper Scissors that I mentioned in a previous chapter. I travel the world extensively sharing testimony of my survival and mentoring young woman who have experienced some kind of trauma in their lives.

How can I help them see the light if I refuse to step out of the darkness? I wholeheartedly believe that the enemy wants us to remain stuck so that we cannot help others get freedom. This book is just another tool that God is using to set the captives free. Many of you are no longer victims or prisoners of people. You are in bondage to the pain of your past because you are not willing to just release it.

Here is another advantage, your mental health. I have endured childhood molestation, multiple rapes, betrayal and divorce. My mental health has been in jeopardy since the day I was born into my perfectionist family. The constant fear of failure or the fear of injury is all you can seem to focus on daily. Success creates depression because all you are comfortable with is disappointment. When someone you have finally decided to trust keeps their word every time, you fall into anxiety mode waiting yet and still for them to do what all the others have done, damage you.

It is no surprise to anyone that I struggled with suicidal attempts and thoughts convoluting my mind. Not only did I think I would be better off dead, I thought my family and friends would be better off without me. This was the enemy trying to silence my voice yet again. It did not work. Every day I am awaken to new mercies and I am reminded that I still have a purpose. It is in every day that I get the opportunity to maintain my attitude of forgiveness.

One last benefit is your physical health. Forgiveness promotes health and wholeness. "Out of the heart flows the issues of life."

Fibromyalgia is a condition characterized by chronic pain, fatigue, memory problems and extensive mood changes.

I was diagnosed with this debilitating disease and truly thought my life was over and done. Healing was just on the other side of forgiving my god sister for touching me and making me keep silent. It did not stop there. Remember, it is a constant attitude. I had to walk all through my past and forgive the teacher, the boyfriend, my parents and my spouse. It was not easy, but it was so worth it.

This chapter was purposely titled fragments of forgiveness. The totality of the courage to forgive can be quite overwhelming. If we can do the work piece by piece, then we can experience the benefits of learning to forgive others and ourselves.

Remember forgiveness is for you. It is a choice that only you must be willing to make. It doesn't remove the pain of what happened, but it perpetuates healing from the inside out.

"And I know that nothing good lives in me, that is, in my sinful nature. I want to do what is right, but I can't." (Romans 7:18, NLT) How does this verse encourage you to be willing to forgive yourself and others?

_____

_____

_____

_____

_____

_____

_____

_____

_____

_____

_____

_____

_____

_____

Forgiveness is not an occasional act, it is a constant attitude (Martin Luther King, Jr.) How can you apply this statement to your life?

_____

_____

_____

_____

_____

_____

_____

_____

_____

_____

_____

_____

_____

_____

_____

_____

Shattered Glass

"

He heals
the wounds of every
shattered heart.

Psalm 147:3

Chapter 5
Healing the Hurt

The consequence of forgiveness is healing. Now my friend, here comes the fun parts of seeking healing with our loving God. In this chapter and the chapters after this, I will give you some important keys that I continually use to process, reflect, and apply to my everyday life.

News flash, healing does not happen overnight. It is a multi-layered process where our intentionality meets the miraculous powers of

Jesus. It is a daily statement of affirmation that simply says, "Yes, I can." I can be whole and holy. I can live righteously in God's presence, because I am seeking His face and receiving His grace.

After going through the process and identifying any denial, grief, loss, and all that encompasses what could make you need to start some healing work, my recommendation is to find a safe space to do this work. Ask your Heavenly Father for guidance. It will look and feel different for each person, but there typically are key correlations to all counseling, groups, and programs that minister about recovery or healing work. There should be accountability and biblical principles being applied to inspire change.

For the sake of this chapter, I will be speaking on what accountability looks like for the healing work that has been done and what God is doing currently in my life.

We know that God's word speaks specifically to not doing life alone. While I have your attention at this moment, I want to encourage you to build a tribe of people. These are family and friends who will surround you with truth and want to see you succeed in life. Find positive leaders and role models that you look up to that will not just give you loving encouragement but also tough talks because they don't want you to miss out on what God has for you.

There was a time when I was at what felt like my absolute lowest point. Just starting to mentally process the end of my marriage, my mentor and spiritual mother said something I will not ever forget, "I'm not going to coddle you. You can sit in this or you can get up, do the work (healing), and keep going."

Her words shocked me to my core. But just like a patient in cardiac arrest, those words brought my heart back into rhythm. My initial reaction was to resist and retaliate. Didn't she know that I was in an extremely vulnerable and raw place in my life? My life was falling apart and all I wanted to hear was something that was going to make me feel better. This did not make me feel better, but neither does the patient after their heart has been shocked back into rhythm by the defibrillator. The goal was to restore life, by any means necessary.

This is exactly what God had brought her into my life to do. When she and I initially connected, we both agreed on the tone of our relationship. I would honor her wholeheartedly, love her unconditionally and submit to her mentorship. God sent me a whole pit bull in the spirit. She speaks the truth to me in love and she has never coddled me, not once. Why? Because that is not what I needed. My life was on the line here and I needed someone that was going to get violent in the spirit for me and with me.

The idea and concept of mentorship was first presented to us in the bible. Jesus had twelve men that he labeled as disciples. They traveled with Him from city to city performing miracles. He taught them regularly on the things of the kingdom. They addressed Jesus as teacher, master, Lord and Father. Following Jesus and being His disciple did not always come with great perks. There were times when you would experience attempts on your life. Fast forward to now, I mean it would be pretty cool today to say you were there when He opened blinded eyes or made limbs to grow. How cool would it have been to be there when He fed five thousand people with two fish and five loaves of bread and they had twelve baskets of leftovers? He gave them a command, **"greater works than these will you do," (John 14:12, KJV, emphasis added).** Imagine the kind of accountability the twelve experienced with Jesus as their mentor and leader.

Another form of accountability can be found within your peer groups. The bible says that, **"Iron sharpens iron; so a man sharpeneth the countenance of his friend," (Proverbs 27:17, KJV).** Pray for God to send people who are willing to walk alongside you in your journey of healing. These are people or a person, who may be going through very similar, if not the very same, life experiences as you and are seeking healing in their lives as well.

To do the deep, heavy heart work, you must be willing to become vulnerable with these people. Many might view it as weakness, but the power to be vulnerable is an expression of great strength. Jesus exampled vulnerability when his friend Lazarus died. Although He knew that in a matter of moments He would rise again, **"Jesus wept," (John 11:35, KJV).** It is the shortest verse in scripture, but also the most thought-provoking scripture.

Whether you have a single mentor or group of peers, both require the ability to be vulnerable coupled with a personal relationship with Jesus. We can have the accountability, but nothing is more relevant to your healing than having Jesus living on the inside of you. This relationship is the most important of all the love relationships that we have. This would include having the courage to be honest with God about you. In case you missed it, He is all knowing so He knows it before you have ever commenced to the act. He knows every thought before we think it and has already numbered our steps before we ever move in one direction or another. God knows you better than you know you.

Hear me sis, there is nothing God desires more for us than wholeness in every area of our lives. However, He will not force His will upon you and me. It has to be something that we want from Him. **"Take delight in the Lord, and he will**

give you the desires of your heart," (Psalms 37:4, NIV).

I wanted it badly. I needed it just that much more. I have a daughter who is depending on me and a generation of woman who are in desperate need of not just my survival but my healing. That is why having someone like my spiritual mom in my life was imperative. She allowed me the space to be vulnerable, but not the option to be weak.

I also, highly recommend building a tribe of the same gender. Seriously, mine is like no other. These women have walked with me through some of the toughest seasons in my life. Finding the right group meant spending a lot of time in prayer, fasting and spiritual discernment. Not everyone is assigned to you and you are not assigned to everybody. Just because you have an opinion does not mean you have the unction to function.

You are going to share some deeply wounded areas with these people, and you do not need anyone causing an infection. Not only is your relationship with Jesus important, be sure that you check their walk as well. **"Can two people walk together without agreeing on the direction?" (Amos 3:3, NLT)**

Really ask yourself that question. It seems like a rhetorical question, but this is your life we are talking about sis. You are fighting to live while they are secretly trying to assassinate you.

As if you haven't already experienced enough of an emotional ride, you are about to take off on a journey like no other. Full exposure will lead to complete healing. Allow yourself to be seen. Take off your mask of "everything is fine." Leading like Jesus means modeling His transparent behavior.

When He wept, He was still all God, but he was all man too.

For my own personal healing, I needed to surround myself with truth-tellers. People who were willing to hear me, love me, but not let me bleed to death. The presence of blood signifies life but bleeding out suggests death. If you are a leader and already have a platform, you can still be bleeding and leading, but it's that transparency that says: *I'm a leader but today, in this moment, I cannot be okay too and work on it.* This my friend is authentic leadership through vulnerability.

Stop expecting people to understand your vulnerability and transparency. Everyone can't handle your pain with care. The revelation of this reality will set you free from years of hurting. It is not your responsibility to make people understand or empathize with you.

Surviving my latest trauma of divorce has me in a very unfamiliar place of vulnerability. Sure, I have friends and accountability partners to coach me through my tough times, but when they are not available, God is always there. He is my constant in the midst of the storm. I truly have learned how to lean and depend on Him.

Allow me the space to be completely honest and transparent with you all, healing is hard. Have you ever experienced a broken bone? Well, let me just tell you the cause was just the beginning of the pain. Depending on what was broken, you might need surgery and maybe even some rehabilitation. However, every doctor will tell you that the pain will get worse before it ever starts to get better. The goal isn't to just restore functionality, but it is to improve and increase the strength of the bone.

You, me, we have gone through some major tragedies. Some that many people did not survive, but we did. As I mentioned before, I was diagnosed with fibromyalgia. That is one debilitating disease and God thought I was strong enough to endure it. I had thirteen surgeries in the span of five years. As a result, there was daily struggles with anxiety and depression. All of these things impacted my career, my calling and even my personal growth.

Please recognize that I said impacted not obliterated those areas. These were some tough seasons in my life, but I prevailed. My faith leveled up and my platform for ministry evolved. Although there were setbacks, they became setups for my future. What the enemy meant to destroy me; God used it to promote me. John 10:10 says, **"The thief's purpose is to steal and kill and destroy. My purpose is to give them a rich and satisfying life." (NLT)**

Another facet of my healing was the continual soul cleansing. This consisted of taking daily inventory to remove any feelings, thoughts, desires and maybe even people who were not properly aligned with my purpose and destiny. Sometime those people would include family members, close friends and even ministry partners.

This daily inventory required a commitment to prayer and my willingness to do the hard stuff. I had to be willing to present everything to him and ask, "is this really for me?" The next step required obedience, even with difficult things.

It isn't easy walking away from your family and close friends. These are the people who were supposed to be there for you in the good and bad times. The hardest soul ties to break are those with our family. I know I have gone back to God and asked again, and that is okay sis. The objective is your healing not to create more hurt.

God has a major plan for your life. **"For I know the plans I have for you, declares the Lord, plans to prosper you and not to harm you, plans to give you hope and a future," (Jeremiah 29:11, NIV).** This scripture details four plans for your life; to prosper you, not harm you, give you hope, and a future. When you are unsure of what stays and what goes, use these four things as a litmus. If there is anything in you, your circle or your thoughts that are not in line with the will of God for your life, IT MUST GO.

I want to encourage you to start doing a daily inventory. At the end of each week, do a weekly inventory. It might seem burdensome in the beginning, but I promise you within 30 days you will begin to experience freedom like no other. Now, you are able to do a monthly inventory. I would even dare to believe that some of you will be healed physically as well as emotionally.

You might be thinking, Kristal I have no idea how to even start doing this daily inventory. Below I have included some questions that will help you get started on the inventory.

1. Were there things I thought or ways I acted out throughout my day that were not reflective of Christ?

2. Did I experience any worries or fears that made me want to escape, shut down, or detach?

3. Did I indulge in any false beliefs of myself or others?

4. How did I fair in using my "Greater is He" strength? How did I do at resisting any temptation that I faced in the day?

5. How can I be better tomorrow or next time?

Shattered Glass

Do you think it is important to have people in your life that make you better? Make a list of people that you would include or are already in your tribe.

Start your daily inventory today. Choose one of the questions listed in this chapter and answer below.

_____

_____

_____

_____

_____

_____

_____

_____

_____

_____

_____

_____

_____

Healing the Hurt

"

Chin up, sis!
You're not struggling,
you're transitioning!

Kristal Clark

Chapter 6

Getting Unstuck

Remember what my spiritual mom said to me, "I'm not going to coddle you. You can sit in this or you can get up, do the work (healing), and keep going." It still triggers me when I say, read or even type those words. But as jolting as those words were, they shifted the trajectory of my life. She was right, I could stay in this position and situation or I could decide today to take one step forward towards my healing. Instead of focusing on what was wrong, I became intentional about moving forward.

My spiritual vision became less blurred and I started to recognize that I had been in this position and place called stuck for quite a long time. Stuck is a city in the state of Denial. No one really wants to live there, but they can't seem to find the strength or the courage to leave. It is a crowded but lonely and unproductive place. This was my reality.

Every day I am grateful for those words. They changed my mind and therefore, changed my position. We don't want to have the tough conversations and hear the reality of where we are. You are stuck! If you are wondering why you feel like the ground around you is sinking, quit questioning it and move sis.

Getting stuck is one thing but staying stuck is a whole other thing. You might get your car stuck in a ditch, but you don't leave it there. No! You call the tow truck and have them use the necessary tools to get you out of the ditch. This is the same concept with your life.

When you have the proper tools and equipment you can do all things. Yes, that includes getting unstuck from your past, forgiving and healing. My friend you have got to want it bad enough.

Grief and loss won't always look like a physical death of a person. In many cases, grief and loss comes from things like a failed relationship, career, life path, or it could very well be the loss of a loved one. All are equally difficult and can penetrate the soul deeply affecting a person.

I personally do not know of anyone who has not experienced some form of grief. It could be the death of a loved one, a health crisis or even the loss of a job. Whatever the matter might be, grief is universal and does not discriminate.

Grief is like a tidal wave that continuously crashes over you. It also has a way of teaching you some valuable life lessons. You will learn patience with God and the things that He wants to do in your life. Listen sis, loss hurts but God restores.

Contrarily, unprocessed grief can easily become a barrier between you and your healing. Toxic relationships and soul ties are often the result of unprocessed grief. When you block out emotions and fail to deal with the hard things in life, you welcome unhealthy habits that lead to more hurting and pain.

God is the creator of time. Therefore, time responds to His commands. My entire life I have heard, "time heals all wounds." Well time passes and I was still painfully wounded. Then I got the revelation that God heals all wounds when we bring them to Him.

Remember, He heals them not removes them. He will indeed take the pain away, but the healed wound will remain. I believe that all great stories have visual aids. Your wounds, the memories, and scars are just that.

Everyone will process grief differently. With accountability, the process can produce growth. I know you are thinking about how difficult it will be and how it will feel processing the losses. I know, I experienced those same thoughts of fear. But let me tell you, His grace is sufficient. It was enough to get me through the toughest of times and sleepless nights.

It was enough to hold me up when all I wanted to do was collapse on the floor and cry.

It was enough when I wanted to throw in the towel and surrender in defeat.

It was in my weakness that His strength was made perfect. I had to become weak and surrender my will to say yes to His will for my life. That meant feeling every ounce of the pain, not for me but for you.

I have included some steps that will help you navigate the process of grief. These are the exact steps I took and continue to take every single day. Read them, pray about it and then proceed. Seek to balance these five steps so that you are not overwhelmed and give up too quickly. God is the healer, but healing is your responsibility.

- **Pray and ask God to guide your path while you navigate a season of grief and loss.**

- **Find a church home and seek Pastoral Care: counseling, coaching. (Most churches have a ministry dedicated specifically to this.)**

- Attend a recovery group like Celebrate Recovery, one that uses biblical principles in their recovery methods.

- Through the methods above, seek mentorship from a person of the same gender, who is connected to a church and is mature in their recovery similar to what you're working on. Build a connection. Share and listen to their wisdom and advice.

- Seek counseling, preferably a Christian counselor that uses biblical principles.

Where in your life do you have unprocessed grief?

Choose a step from the chapter and discuss how you can begin to take that step in your personal pursuit of healing

_____

_____

_____

_____

_____

_____

_____

_____

_____

_____

_____

_____

_____

_____

_____

95

"

Not all storms come to disrupt
your life. Some come to

clear your path.

Kristal Clark

97

Chapter 7

Moving Forward

Have you ever observed the posture of an athlete? They stand tall, shoulders back and have a confident look on their faces. Their posture and position reflect their confidence.

Personally, I am not much of a sports enthusiast, but my daughter is an athlete. She plays volleyball and she is confidently good at that sport. Sitting in the stands, I often watch her, and her teammates play an obviously much better opponent with so much confidence. They don't enter the competition with a defeated posture. Nope, they enter that gym expecting to win every single time. These girls have been properly conditioned to have a winner's mindset.

That is the same mindset you need to develop. The fact that you have survived is indicative of your ability to win. You have experienced some serious opponents and major setbacks. Nonetheless, here you are. Ponder this, how are you going to celebrate your victory or survival?

In the previous chapter the idea of getting unstuck was presented. Moving forward is the proper response for getting unstuck. Once the tow truck pulls the vehicle form the ditch, he does not leave it there. The point of getting it out of the ditch was so that the driver could get back on track continue moving forward in their journey to their destination.

There is some place you have to be and the only way to get there is if you keep moving forward. **"I have not achieved it, but I focus on this one thing: Forgetting the past and looking forward to what lies ahead," (Philippians 3:13, NLT).** You cannot focus on your past and be present. Be like Paul and forget the past and look forward. Don't focus on the ditch I just pulled you out of or you will find yourself in another one.

The past can either be a distraction or a lesson. You have to make the decision to focus on it or learn from it. The decision was simple for me, I picked up the pieces of my past and used it to learn a valuable lesson. God is the same yesterday, but He does not live there. I wanted to be wherever He was. That meant I had to, **"Forget about what's happened; don't keep going over old history. Be Alert, be present. I'm about to do something brand-**

new. It's bursting out! Don't you see it,"
(Isaiah 43:18–19, MSG)?

God was about to do something brand new in
my life and I wanted to be fully present. This
meant positioning myself to spend time in His
presence. We all have very busy schedules with
our kids, careers and church obligations. But I
was on the verge of my next level. I had to
become intentional about spending time with
God.

My commitment would determine how God
was going to move me forward. I wanted to go all
the way, so my mind was fully made up. I wanted
everything He had for me. I established a routine
and developed a mindset that positioned me to
spend quality time with God. I did not just want
to give Him what was left over after carpool,
corporate meetings and family dinner. God

wanted intimate time with me and that is exactly what I gave Him.

My priority became properly positioning myself to hear and recognize His voice. This would require silencing all other voices that had been the controlling authority in my life. In the beginning, it was difficult to completely shut off and shut down the world around. After a while, I begin to look forward to my dates with Jesus. Our time together was better than incredible, and the evidence was being displayed in every area of my life.

In our time together, I learned to be specific in my prayer requests. I became like David, **"Create in me a clean heart, O God. Renew a loyal spirit within me" (Psalms 51:10, NLT).** Another word for renew is repair. My spirit had been broken time and time again. It was in need of repair. The damage was seemingly beyond repair. It required the expertise and the work of a specialist. Who better than to take it to the creator, my creator?

My value felt lost. As soon as I became just weak enough to lean on the Father, the repair begins. The world said I was done and was ready to haul me off to the junk yard. I was like an abandon house, ready to be condemned. But God spoke to me very clearly, "Kristal, I add more value to your life because your heart is clean, not because you have a ring."

This was another one of those moments where I felt completely taken aback. I had poured my heart and soul into a man and a marriage and you are telling me that it was for nothing at all? He responded, "Absolutely not. This was all for my glory and your good."

This would have moved most of you to immediately think, wow God is getting glory out of my suffering. Well that is exactly what did not happen. These were hard sayings. I have just lost the very thing that I valued most and found value in and now you are saying that it was all for your glory and my good. I demanded clarity on those statements.

God always confirms His words with the Word. Much like Jacob, I refused to leave our date without a definitive and acceptable explanation. Suddenly, like a light bulb, I remembered the words of Paul. "All things work together for your good."

My heart became so full and overwhelmed with joy and weeping was my only response to His words. He also reminded me of a verse in Isaiah, "I will give you beauty for your ashes." Those words shifted something down on the inside of me and I regained my composure. I knew in that very moment; I was going to survive this and anything that the enemy tried to aim at me.

There was no way I would ever get stuck again. I am plowing ahead full force with holy confidence that no weapon formed against me shall prosper. I am more than a conqueror through Christ Jesus, and I can absolutely do all things through Christ who strengthens me.

The devil tried to take me out before my time, but he failed. He tried to break me, he failed at that too. Then he tried to steal my worth. Yep, you know it, he failed again. He will continue to fail because I am moving forward in my destiny with the blessed assurance that God is getting the glory and it is all working for my good. **"And I am certain that God, who began the good work within you, will continue his work until it is finally finished on the day when Christ Jesus returns" (Philippians 1:6, NLT).**

Shattered Glass

What is keeping you from Moving Forward in your journey of healing?

_____

_____

_____

_____

_____

_____

_____

_____

_____

_____

_____

_____

_____

_____

_____

_____

_____

Seek God for verses of scripture to encourage your decision to Move Forward. Write them below.

_____

_____

_____

_____

_____

_____

_____

_____

_____

_____

_____

_____

_____

_____

_____

_____

"

She made broken look beautiful
and strong look invincible, she
walked with the universe on her
shoulders and made it look like

a pair of wings.

Unknown

Chapter 8

Starting Over

Whoever said starting over was easy to do obviously had never done it before. There was nothing at all easy about having to begin again. Nonetheless, my healing required a new beginning. That is what restoration is all about, returning something to a former owner, place or condition.

As you already know, I walked through some life altering events. What a blessing to know that God offers us the opportunity to just start over. We do not have to remain in our condition unless we choose to stay there. What I so love about God is this fact, even if we made the decision to continue, His love would remain right there. Let me tell you the truth, God does not want us to get stuck in a season.

Starting over became less about being broken and more about becoming whole. The decision started in my mind. The great apostle Paul writes, **"Do not conform to the pattern of this world but be transformed by the renewing of your mind" (Romans 12:2, NIV).** When you make up your mind to get healed and be better, then transformation can and will begin to happen. No one could make the decision for me. I had to be the one to reach for God's hand to pull me out of the hole that I was making my dwelling place.

The negative thoughts of insecurity and inadequacy had me covered in shame and self-pity. There were moments that I would spiral into depression and begin replaying the trauma of my childhood and the betrayal in my adulthood. Suddenly, there were suicidal thoughts. I could just end it all right here, right now. The enemy will make you think that taking your own life will give you joy. It is for this very reason we have to learn to renew our minds daily with the word of God.

The devil is a liar that **"comes to kill, steal and to destroy you, but Jesus has come that you might have life and life in abundance"** (John10:10, emphasis added). Jesus said, **"I am the way, the truth and the light" (John 14:6, NLT).**

As soon as my divorce was finalized, God commanded I leave where I was and go into what I would consider a foreign land. Many have questioned my decision to make such an enormous move, but I was obedient to the voice of the Lord. I know it might seem foolish to be in a strange land, **"But God chose the foolish things of the world to shame the wise; God chose the weak things of the world to shame the strong" (1 Corinthians 1:27, NIV).**

After all I have endured, I appeared to the enemy and so many around me as weak. The love of God is the grace of God, **"His grace is sufficient for me, and His power is made perfect in weakness. Therefore, I will boast all the more gladly about my weaknesses, so that Christ's power may rest on me" (2 Corinthians 12:9, KJV, emphasis added).** This is a unique season that I am in, but I am so grateful to be able to walk through it with His sufficient grace and power. **"That is why, for the sake of Christ, I delight in weaknesses, in**

insults, in hardships, in persecutions, in difficulties. For when I am weak, then I am strong" (2 Corinthians 12:10, KJV).

Every ounce of what I have endured, happened to me and for you. You are reading this book because God trusted me to be hurt, broken and mishandled. He trusted me to be sitting right here sharing my story with you and so many around the world so that they too could become an overcomer. **"The righteous person may have many troubles, but the Lord delivers him from them all" (Psalms 34:19, NIV).** Thank God I have been delivered. He not only rescued me from my oppressors, but He also liberated my mind. He has given me a peace that is so great. **"And the peace of God, which transcends all understanding, will guard your hearts and your minds in Christ Jesus" (Philippians 4:7, NIV).**

In my journey of heartbreak, I have learned to keep my mind focused on God. **"You will keep in perfect peace those whose minds are steadfast, because they trust in you" (Isaiah 26:3, NIV)** If I were to just allow myself to replay the sexual, physical, mental and emotional abuse over and over, I would be insane. Of course, that is what the enemy wants us to do. He wants us to concentrate on the problem and not seek after the problem solver.

This reminds me of a story in the bible. We all know Peter the brave rebel. He was given clearance to walk on water. As long as he was focused on his destination, Jesus, he was successful. As soon as he lost focus, he started to sink. Listen friend, whatever you do, do not take your eyes off of Jesus and lose your focus.

What if David had focused on the roar of the lion and the growl of the bear? He would have never slayed Goliath. You have giants in your life, and they are tormenting you and mocking the God you serve. David's unwavering courage is always encouraging to me. This young boy accepting the challenge that so many adults cowardly rejected. He was willing to defend His God and their people.

Even as a child David was a foreshadowing of the Messiah. He was willing to risk his own life to save the lives of others. We all know how the story ends, David was victorious. This is exactly how my story ends and your story will end the same way. Why? Because Jesus did not risk His life; He gave His life so that we could live. In His resurrection we are also raised to a new life in Him. **"Surely God is my salvation; I will trust and not be afraid. For the Lord God is my strength and my song, and He also has become my salvation" (Isaiah 12:2, NIV).**

But what happens when you have passion but also a lot of broken pieces that needed to be dealt with? I had to be okay with starting again after ending my marriage and trusting that God has the outcome: the ending and all the glory. I had to stop focusing on my pain and letting it cripple me as I thought about my God sister abusing me. I thought about when I allowed my personal safety to be compromised as I made myself believe that being with the "cool kids" was where I was happiest when this was exactly what contributed to more of my sexual brokenness.

Trust Is Key

One of the final keys is trusting God. I realized that even though I know God is in control, I still had this desire to control. I had to release it, continually, daily. My heart's prayer to Him was to release it. For God to dictate what's in my heart to know what to do and to abide in His will for myself, my life, and my calling. And let me tell you, it is a struggle. Stepping out of control looks so much different especially in the ways I wanted to control. Stepping out of control is a vulnerable place, and it is uncomfortable. What it looks like in my life is me being okay with knowing that God answers prayers that are in His will and His timing. It is also the realization that I'm affecting my relationship with God and His plans when I don't let Him fully drive or guide me in everything I do. Do you not "see" what God is doing? He said He is doing a new thing in your life, but the old has to go, to make room for the new to come. You may have thought that the old was the best you'll ever get, but God knows your life from beginning to end. Therefore, He knows if you're settling or if now is not the right time. New joy, new peace, new contentment, new anointing. I am not losing anything but instead, I am getting something new and fresh. You have to speak this over yourself when the urge to take the reins bubbles up. It's your choice, but in order to achieve the newness with God, your trust in Him is key.

So, you may be asking, how do you give yourself over to trusting Him over your own abilities. I'd like to share something very personal that I'm believing will be an essential key in unlocking your healing and growth in your relationship with God. I know this helped me tremendously. God gave me a declaration statement for my life, and I'm sharing it with you. Something that I speak over myself to remind myself of what He says and what He has for me.

I will be all that God has called me to be. I will walk with Him through all of my brokenness, pains and newness. I will trust Him with all of my heart as I make Him the priority in my life. I will lean not to my own understanding as I walk in healing from insecurities, sexual brokenness, low self-esteem, seeking approval, and fear and abandonment. I won't stop. I will push no matter what it looks or feels like. I will be whole emotionally. I will be whole spiritually.

I am equipped to fight the devil head on with no hesitation. I will embrace who the kingdom is calling. My attitude will reflect gratitude, compassion, mentorship, and discipleship. For He is doing a new thing in me.

God is doing a new thing in you—sit in His presence and ask Him for your declaration statement for your life. You're more than welcome to use mine, but I know that God has specific words for you and I challenge you to seek Him and receive them.

If Starting Over was possible today, what would that look life for you? Would you relocate? Get new friends? Switch Careers? (Be specific)

_____

_____

_____

_____

_____

_____

_____

_____

_____

_____

_____

_____

_____

_____

Write your own declarations. What are things that you are trusting God to do in your life.

_____

_____

_____

_____

_____

_____

_____

_____

_____

_____

_____

_____

_____

_____

_____

Epilogue

I leave you with this beautifully written word by Kiersten Lewis. Let it sink in and bless you.

No one ever expects it to happen,

but when it does, it comes with a blow.

Where It knocks you off your feet,

and it leaves you breathless.

Wondering how could this be so?

And soon, the very thing you've been trying to hold together

Becomes exposed.

And soon everyone knows.

Everyone sees.

Sure some stay, but the majority go.

But your just left there,

Looking at the shattered pieces on the floor,

Not really knowing what to do.

You want to move on, but you can't.

Because you're blinded,

By regret, hurt, unforgiveness.

You're not sure which direction to go,

so you stop and begin to wonder why.

Why did this happen to me?

Why wasn't I enough?

Why am I the one hurting, and they're not?

Why do I have to do this alone?

Soon the why's begun to add up.

You become trapped, stuck,

Dead inside,

Not really living,

Just existing,

And you begin to realize,

you've come to an end.

But what if the end is really just the beginning,

And what looks lifeless is actually God trying to breathe in new life.

What if it's in the fragments and shattered pieces of glass, where God begins to piece together a different story?

Where He takes all the hurt, the abuse, the heartache

And intricately puts it back together, but not in a way it was before,

In a new way where it's stronger, bolder,

And what may have looked like ruins

Were in fact the very things He's using to rebuild,
remold, and recreate you.

And what the enemy may have meant for bad,

God will use for good.

Sure you're not as smooth as glass like before,

But whatever you put in the master's hands,

He can make it beautiful.

He can restore it.

He can redeem it.

He can forgive it.

He can heal it.

All the shattered pieces,

He can use it . . .

"

Turn your wounds
into wisdom.

Unknown

Appendix

List the lies that you've been believing about yourself, your life, and your relationships below.

Lie:

_____

_____

_____

Truth:

_____

_____

_____

Lie:

_____

_____

_____

Truth:

_____

_____

_____

Lie:

_____

_____

_____

Truth:

_____

_____

_____

Lie:

_____

_____

_____

Truth:

_____

_____

_____

Appendix

"For I know the plans I have for you, declares the Lord, plans to prosper you, not to harm you. Plans to give you hope and a future."

–Jeremiah 29:11

"I praise you because I am fearfully and wonderfully made, your works are wonderful, I know that full well."

–Psalm 139:4

"No weapon formed against you shall prosper ..."

–Isaiah 54:17

"The Lord will make you the head, not the tail."

–Deuteronomy 28:13

Plan Your Date with Jesus

Date Details (Time, Length, Location):

_____

_____

_____

What is the agenda for the date? (pray, read scripture, worship)

_____

_____

_____

_____

What are you expecting from your time spent with Jesus?

_____

_____

_____

_____

Appendix

The last few pages are lined and left blank.

Use this space to start writing your healing story.

Appendix

_____

_____

_____

_____

_____

_____

_____

_____

_____

_____

_____

_____

_____

_____

_____

_____

_____

_____

_____

Appendix

_____

_____

_____

_____

_____

_____

_____

_____

_____

_____

_____

_____

_____

_____

_____

_____

_____

_____

Appendix

Appendix

Connect with Kristal Clark

- Website:

WWW.KRISTALCLARK.COM

WWW.KRISTALCLARKSPEAKS.COM

- Connect with Kristal Clark on Social Media:

    - **Facebook:** @KristalClarkSpeaks

    - **Instagram:** Kristal Clark

We look forward to connecting with you!

Made in the USA
Columbia, SC
25 January 2020